FARNBOROUGH
HALL

Warwickshire

**National
Trust**

Acknowledgements

The late Gervase Jackson-Stops's guide of 1981 has been revised by Jeffrey Haworth, and then again by Simon Chesters Thompson of the National Trust in 2015. The Trust is indebted to the late Sir Howard Colvin for the transcript of William Perritt's bill of 1750; Mrs Sarah Markham for the extracts from the travel diaries of her ancestor, John Loveday the antiquary; Dr H. Oehler of the University of Cologne for the use of his notes on the antique sculpture; Mr A. C. Wood for information about the carver Benjamin King, and the masons Richard Newman and William Hiorns; and Mr H. W. Hawkes for information about the architect Sanderson Miller. Mr and the late Mrs Geoffrey Holbech, and the late Mr E. K. Day kindly assisted in many ways.

Sources

The primary published source for the history of Farnborough is the account given by Gordon Nares in *Country Life* (11 and 18 February 1954). Some of the family papers are deposited in Warwickshire Record Office, where Lady Newdigate's travel journal is also to be found (among the Arbury papers). The account of a visit in 1746 is given by the anonymous author of *Hypomnemata*, a manuscript in the British Library (Add. MSS 6230). A detailed account of the sculpture collection was published in Germany in 1995.

Photographs: National Gallery of Canada, Ottawa pp. 12–13; National Trust p. 20 (top); NT/Robert Anderson pp. 29, 30; National Trust Images; Matthew Antrobus front cover, p. 27 (top), Andrew Butler pp. 2, 6-7, 9, 10, 11, 14, 15, 17, 20 (bottom), 24, 25, 26, back cover, Angelo Hornak pp. 18, 31 (top), Chris Lacey pp. 19, 23, 27 (bottom), Nick Meers p. 31 (bottom), David Sellman p. 5; Royal Commission on the Historical Monuments of England pp. 1, 28; Warwickshire County Record Office (2403u) p. 22.

High-quality prints from the extensive and unique collections of National Trust Images are available at www.ntprints.com

© 1999 National Trust
Reprinted 2003, revised 2010, 2015
ISBN 978-1-84359-077-4
Registered charity no. 205846
Birds eye map by Andy Bates of Bates Fine Art-design Limited
Designed and typeset by James Shurmer
Printed by Acorn Press, Swindon, for National Trust Enterprises Ltd, Heelis, Kemble Drive, Swindon, Wilts SN2 2NA
on Cocoon Silk made from 100% recycled paper

CONTENTS

Introduction   *page* 4

Tour of the House   8

The Interior   8

   The Hall   8

   The Drawing Room or Saloon   10

   The Staircase   14

   The Library   16

The Exterior   17

   The West Front   18

   The North and South Fronts   19

   The Coach-house and Stable Block   20

   The Old Kitchen   20

The Terrace Walk   21

   William Holbech's Terrace Walk and   21
    Roman-Style Countryside

   The Ionic Temple   24

   The Oval Pavilion   24

   The Obelisk   26

   The Game Larder   27

   Granny's Walk   27

The Holbech Family   28

FARNBOROUGH HALL

Ambrose Holbech of Mollington bought Farnborough in 1683 from the Raleighs, and here his descendants live still. His son William probably began to reconstruct the old house after marrying Elizabeth Alington in 1692. Their arms and entwined initials appear on the richly worked ceiling of the Staircase, and they rebuilt the west side of the house with its large windows closely spaced, perhaps intending this up-to-date work as a smart new entrance front. Their son, also William, succeeded his father in 1717 and in his long reign until 1771 had ample time to adapt the rest of the house, with dignity outside and richness within, to purchase fine furnishings and sculpture, which survive, and to create one of the most poetic of English landscapes: it is adorned by water, three surviving temples and an obelisk.

Family tradition has young William disappointed in love consoling himself with a sojourn in Italy of a decade or more: he was seen in Florence late in 1732 or early 1733, in Rome later that year and (with his younger brother Hugh) the following March. By the end of April 1734, the brothers were in Venice, and, according to Col. Burges, the Resident, on their way home. This is undoubtedly when the three Panini paintings and two of the Canalettos once in the Dining Room were bought (the second pair of Canalettos being commissioned while the artist was in England in 1746–50). The sculptured busts in the Hall and Staircase were bought at this time in Italy. Their incorporation in the internal architecture of the building is part of William Holbech's wish that Farnborough resemble the houses he had seen and loved in Italy. The rich ochre colour of the exterior is also Italian but achieved with the locally quarried Hornton stone, used in contrast with local grey stone enrichments.

William's building campaign was principally of the 1740s, with the completed stucco decoration in the Hall, Drawing Room and Staircase (that in the Library has vanished) invoiced at £434 4s 4d on 14 November 1750. Much of it by a Yorkshireman, William Perritt, it is some of the most spectacular Rococo plasterwork in England. Perritt also decorated the once-famous rotunda of 1742 at Ranelagh pleasure gardens, designed by a London architect, William Jones. It is likely William Holbech's friend and neighbour, the gentleman-architect Sanderson Miller, helped him in his work. The amateur's hand is paramount: bedroom windows at floor level to permit a higher ceiling in the Hall are compensated for by an overall *élan* unusual in a squire's house, and by the inspired decision to make the Hall and Staircase (and once the Library) into sculpture galleries of Roman portrait busts, ancient and modern, but lightly elegant rather than heavily overbearing.

William Holbech's landscaping was on an altogether more elaborate scale, its chief feature being a raised terrace gently rising in an arc from the house and running for three-quarters of a mile, affording long views over the Hanwell valley and the land Holbech owned, and thus creating the effect at least of the Roman *campagna*. The Edwardian laurels grown high cut out some of the visual disturbance, but destroy the clarity and breadth of William's conception. Three of his temples can still be enjoyed: the oval pavilion, the Ionic temple and the obelisk; the fourth and most elaborate temple, 'in the form of a pentagon, two stories high, with a balcony on top', had vanished by the end of the eighteenth century.

Most of the estate was sold in 1948, following extensive damage in the gales of 1947. The house, with 344 acres, passed to the National Trust in 1960, and the principal contents were secured in 1986 and 1988.

The exterior with pink Japanese anemones in the foreground

TOUR OF THE HOUSE

The Interior

THE HALL

The old manor house at Farnborough may have in part dictated the design of the present building, with this room following the outline of an earlier great hall. The front door leads into one end, and the Drawing Room door opposite is an earlier opening in what was once an external wall. The room itself was formed about 1750 by the second William Holbech, and the Classical sculpture ranged round the walls was brought back by him from Italy, which he had visited in his mid-thirties. Marble busts of Roman emperors and Classical goddesses are placed in shallow oval niches, supported on elaborate plasterwork brackets (in some cases adapted as overdoors), while above the windows and the deep niches opposite are portrait medallions in low-relief.

SCULPTURE

As in many eighteenth-century collections of sculpture, the pieces acquired by William Holbech are a mixture of antique and some contemporary Roman work. Most of the early examples have been extensively restored, or heads have been fitted to alien (but still antique) shoulders. William Holbech had a particular predilection for medallions or *tondi*, obviously thinking of their decorative effect: the two flanking the chimneypiece were formed by splitting an antique head and setting it within new oval mounts.

DECORATION

What is most remarkable about the sculpture at Farnborough is the way that it has been incorporated into a unified Palladian scheme of decoration, rarely found in other English country houses, save the very grandest such as Holkham or Petworth. Matthew Brettingham's galleries for the Earls of Leicester and Egremont were also conceived a full decade after William Holbech's.

PLASTERWORK

Although confined within strictly geometrical compartments, the plasterwork of the ceiling is in exuberant Rococo style with garlands of roses and celandine among the ornament in the central sections, and masks of Diana and Bacchus in cartouches at each end. The plasterer responsible for this, and probably for similar work at Ecton in Northamptonshire, was the Yorkshire-born craftsman William Perritt, whose bill was settled by Holbech in 1750.

FIREPLACE

The overmantel with a bold broken pediment is carved in wood with festoons of flowers, probably by Benjamin King from Warwick, while the stone chimneypiece below is carved in the same style, with swirling acanthus foliage and a pierced Rococo shell at the centre.

FLOOR AND DOORS

The floor is unusual in that it exactly repeats the arrangement of the ceiling panels, with the pattern rendered in dark and light flagstones. The six beautiful mahogany doors preserve their original brass handles and lock plates.

(Previous page) The south front

The Hall

PICTURE

IN OVERMANTEL:

After PANINI (1691/2–1765?)
*The piazza of St Peter's in Rome with Bernini's
colonnades*
The original (sold in 1929) was another of William
Holbech's purchases in Italy. An unknown antiquary whose journal survives in the British
Museum, and who visited Farnborough in 1746,
records seeing this picture and some of William
Holbech's sculpture already displayed in the house:
'several busts of white marble, one of black; and
two of alto relievos, one of Socrates, and the other
(as it seems) of Lucius Verus, all brought from
Rome'.

FURNITURE

Pair of side-tables with cabriole legs and marble
tops, c.1740. Dr Richard Pococke, who came to
Farnborough in 1756, noticed 'several ancient
busts and very beautiful fineer'd marble tables'.

Pair of upholstered mahogany armchairs, c.1750. They
are of superlative quality, with unusual pierced
legs.

Circular centre-table, early nineteenth-century. It is
inlaid with specimen marbles of different colours
and types. The top was bought in Rome by Sir
John Mordaunt (whose mother was a Holbech) in
1830 and the base made in England by Gillows of
Lancaster.

The Drawing Room or Saloon

PORCELAIN

Pair of enormous Chinese export *famille rose* vases, mid-eighteenth-century.

THE DRAWING ROOM
OR SALOON

If a choice has to be made, this is perhaps the finest interior in the house, with its perfectly balanced Rococo decoration and fine white marble chimneypiece and overmantel. The room was formed within the original courtyard by the second William Holbech, again about 1750, especially to house a series of large views of Venice by Canaletto, together with two paintings of Rome by

Panini. The originals of these pictures were unfortunately sold in 1929 in order to retain the estate and were replaced by copies, but the unity of the room, with its magnificent plasterwork picture frames, and the highly architectural treatment of each of the four walls, has remained undisturbed.

PLASTERWORK

The plasterwork is of the highest order. Although William Perritt's bill for plasterwork in this room survives, much of it is tantalisingly reminiscent of Francesco Vassalli's work at certain Midlands houses such as Hagley. The ceiling, freer than that in the Hall, has an oval central panel surrounded by garlands of flowers in an almost three-dimensional technique. At the four corners are medallions of Roman emperors surmounted by lively dragons or wyverns.

The chimneypiece on the east wall, surmounted by an overmantel with a broken pediment, is balanced on the west wall by a deep niche. Similar broken pediments recur over the niches and doorcases, and, with slightly different scrolling shapes, over the windows, thus tying the decorative elements of the room together. The architraves above the two doors are ornamented with vines, an appropriately Bacchic motif for a dining-room, while panels at the four corners of the room – perhaps the finest work of all – have festoons representing William Holbech's sporting interests, including guns and bows and arrows, and his musical tastes, including horns, flutes, sackbuts and a fully strung violin, all in plaster.

Between the windows is an oval pier-glass set into a frame flanked by urns and surmounted by a large cornucopia of fruit and flowers, all highly asymmetrical and in the advanced Rococo fashion. The Holbech family believes this small area of plasterwork is by Thomas Roberts of Oxford on account of the leaves curling around the glass, as at Kirtlington Park in Oxfordshire. The existence of two large staples in the wall, which may originally have supported a painting or a Linnell mirror (see p. 16) in the original scheme, indicates that William Holbech changed his mind when the rest of the plasterwork had been completed.

PICTURES

The view-paintings themselves provide one of the earliest known instances of pictures set within specially designed plasterwork frames to decorate an entire room. They are also larger in scale than the Canalettos later used by Henry Holland to line the walls of the dining-room at Woburn Abbey in Bedfordshire. The idea was subsequently adopted by Neo-classical architects such as Robert Adam in the Saloon at Nostell Priory or Carr of York in the Harlequin Saloon at Ribston Park, both in Yorkshire.

Two of the Canalettos were probably bought by William Holbech in the 1730s in Venice, where he met the artist. The other two were painted during Canaletto's first visit to England in 1746–50. According to tradition, Canaletto himself chose the Italian craftsmen to carry out the plasterwork surrounds to the paintings, and Mrs Holbech observed that it is subtly different in handling from the rest of Perritt's work. The pair showing the piazza are markedly lower in key than the two nearest the windows, a difference which indeed suggests an earlier dating than their companions. Canaletto would doubtless have brought drawings with him to England, in order to supply Venetian views as required, and one can well imagine

(Right) Ornate Rococo plasterwork surrounds the pier-glass in the Drawing Room

*St Mark's and the Clock Tower, Venice;
by Canaletto (National Gallery of
Canada, Ottawa). One of the paintings
that used to decorate the Drawing Room,
sold in 1929 and replaced by a copy*

William Holbech approaching him for the second pair to complete his decorative scheme for the Drawing Room at just this time. The copies were made by a number of Chinese painters, when the pictures were sold in 1929, and the originals are now in the National Gallery of Canada, the National Gallery of Victoria in Melbourne, the Augsburg Museum in Germany, and a private collection in America.

BETWEEN DOORWAYS:

After PANINI (1691/2–1765?)
Interior of St Peter's, Rome

FIREPLACE WALL:

After CANALETTO (1697–1768)
St Mark's Square, Venice, with the clock tower
Painted from a small drawing now at Windsor Castle.

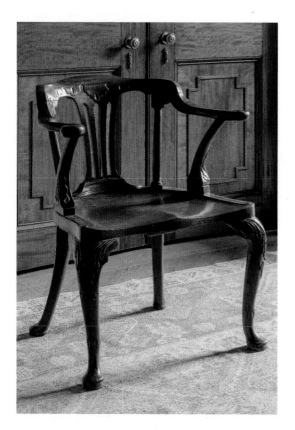

The large mahogany chairs, c.1740, have unusual columnar supports to the low backs

After PANINI (1691/2–1765?)
The Capitol, Rome
With the famous equestrian statue of Marcus Aurelius in the centre of the piazza flanked by Michelangelo's wings.

After CANALETTO (1697–1768)
S. Maria della Salute, Venice, with a stretch of the Grand Canal

WALL OPPOSITE FIREPLACE:

After CANALETTO (1697–1768)
Venice: The Dogana from the Piazzetta
Venice: The base of St Mark's campanile with Sansovino's Library

SCULPTURE

Negro bust, c.1700. This was noted here by a visitor in 1746 and was rescued at auction in recent years.

FURNITURE

Two pairs of Neo-classical side-tables with marble tops, c.1760, in the Chippendale–early Adam style.

THE STAIRCASE

This remains, despite its mid-eighteenth-century skylight dome and wall decoration, substantially as conceived by the first William Holbech, between 1692 and 1705. The lower flight of the oak stairs was damaged by fire in 1926, but has since been reconstructed with fluted balusters and prominent curving handrail, typical of the work of the Smiths of Warwick, local architects who probably built the west front soon after 1701 (see p. 17). The great oval wreath of fruit and flowers in plaster on the ceiling, and the four corner panels bearing the arms and entwined initials of William Holbech and his wife Elizabeth Alington, are also of this early period. The plasterwork is believed to be by Edward Goudge, one of the greatest seventeenth-century plasterers, who also worked at Belton in Lincolnshire and Chatsworth in Derbyshire.

(Right) The Staircase

As first constructed, the Staircase would have had a flat ceiling, and may have been lit by windows on the south and east walls. However, when the second William Holbech came to reconstruct the house in the mid-eighteenth century, such windows were blocked in order to house the Roman sculpture. To compensate, he had the central section of the ceiling, immediately inside the wreath, cut away, and constructed a charming oval skylight dome above (the present filigree glazing bars and coloured glass are Regency). The plasterer responsible for decorating the Hall and Drawing Room, William Perritt, was then employed to decorate the inside of the dome with panels of acanthus and charming rosettes of different shapes, almost like enlarged snowflakes, round its base. He also contributed the plasterwork of the four walls, with more garlands of flowers tied by flowering ribbons, and a broad band of acanthus at first-floor level, with life-like rams' masks in the centre of each.

FLOOR

The stone floor, with small diamond-shaped black flagstones, came from Wilmcote in Warwickshire, according to Mr Holbech's great-uncle, Canon Holbech.

SCULPTURE

RIGHT-HAND WALL:

Lucilla, wife of Emperor Lucius Verus. Probably second-century AD.

CENTRE WALL:

Emperor Lucius Verus (reigned AD 161–9) with the *paludamentum* (military coat) thrown over his shoulder and a sword belt decorated with the figures of Hercules, Diana and Medusa. This is the finest piece of ancient Roman sculpture from William Holbech's collecting in the 1730s and '40s.

LEFT-HAND WALL:

A Roman Lady, c.AD 230. This is a splendidly preserved and characterful portrait.

FURNITURE

Oval looking-glass, one of three supplied to Farnborough by the furniture maker John Linnell (1729–96).

THE LIBRARY

For a house of this size, the library is a large and remarkably fine one. Some of the books have probably been at Farnborough as long as the Holbechs, but the library was enlarged in Victorian times by Archdeacon Charles Holbech (1818–1901), who was a keen collector of books. Among the older books, there is a 1632 edition of Robert Burton's *Anatomy of Melancholy*, as well as surprises like a 1786 book on ballooning, and a book printed in 1658 whose binding contains fragments of one of the earliest books printed in Oxford (1482). Ultimately, however, the library is really as interesting for what it tells us about life in the house of a family of Warwickshire gentry as it is for individual treasures; there are, for example, fascinatingly several volumes with the ticket of a local circulating library called the 'Banburyshire Book Club'.

Although the Library lies behind the first William Holbech's early eighteenth-century west front, and contains a fine Rococo chimneypiece introduced by his son, the room today has an early nineteenth-century atmosphere, due to the bookcases and Regency furniture introduced by his great-grandson, the fourth William Holbech, who succeeded to the house in 1812. William Perritt's original plasterwork decoration in the 'Library and Closet' (which cost as much as that in the Drawing Room) was probably removed at about this date. The green and gold flock wallpaper was given by Mrs Ronald Holbech in 1960.

PICTURES

The family portraits comprise Archdeacon Holbech (above the fireplace) by William Carter, flanked to the right by his wife and to the left by a Nathaniel Dance copy of the Dean of Lichfield (a great-uncle of the Archdeacon).

The west front

The Exterior

Little visual evidence remains of the old manor house lived in by the Sayes and the Raleighs, unless it is in the thickness of some of the interior walls of the present house and the nearby stable block. But their building must have been of a reasonable size, for in the hearth tax returns of 1663 it was listed as having eleven fireplaces – as against 47 at Warwick Castle, and nine at the house then lived in by the Holbechs at Mollington.

The present house is built of the same dark honey-coloured local Hornton stone, supplies of which are now largely exhausted. Paler ashlar known as Warwickshire Grey is used for the quoins and the door and window dressings. The roof, which is of slate, has been entirely redone in four phases, finishing in 2012, but reusing a great many of the old slates.

At first glance, the present house appears to be all of one date. It is only by walking round to the garden side of the house and comparing the balanced composition of the north and south fronts, both horizontal in emphasis, with the closer-spaced windows, string course and central segment-headed doorway of the west front, that two distinct phases of building become apparent.

THE WEST FRONT

The west front probably dates from soon after 1701, when the first William Holbech succeeded his father, Ambrose, and is thought to have been intended to be a new entrance front for the old manor house, most of which still stood behind it. The window surrounds with their distinctive keystones and the slightly projecting central bay, with a heavy segmental pediment over the doorcase, are typical of the work of William and Francis Smith, the Warwick builders who enjoyed a virtual monopoly in this part of the world during the first quarter of the eighteenth century. A particularly close parallel, with the same contrasting ironstone and ashlar, can be found at Abington near Northampton, which the Smiths built about 1738–43. The attic floor and the balustrade and central gable are, however, additions of the 1740s, made by the second William Holbech to tie this façade in with his new north and south fronts.

The rooms behind the west front were largely redecorated in the late Georgian period, when the slender glazing bars of the windows must also have been introduced, replacing thicker sashes. The handsome lead rainwater heads are original, however, and display the Holbech arms ('vert six escallops, three, two and one argent') beneath the crest 'a maunch vert semée of escallops argent'.

The west front around 1860; watercolour by Mary Holbech

18

The north front

THE NORTH AND SOUTH
FRONTS

The second William Holbech retained his father's
west front, but completely remodelled the rest of
the old manor house in the 1740s, giving it a new
entrance front facing north, and another new
façade to the south taking advantage of the view.
The two differ in details and in the proportions of
their windows, but are nevertheless thought to
have been built at the same time, about 1749, to
the designs of Sanderson Miller. The effect of the
north front, probably largely a recasing of existing
structures, is more monumental than the south,
with the central five bays deeply recessed between
the end 'pavilions', whose return walls are decorated with pairs of niches. On the other side of

the house it appears a more ambitious operation
took place, including the enclosure of a courtyard
to form the present Drawing Room. This only
became clear in 1982, when the casing of the deep
doorway between this room and the Hall was tem-
porarily removed to reveal a keystone of *c*.1700,
decorated with an open daisy-like flower and
clearly once part of an external doorway from the
Hall.

The second William Holbech thus made the
south front symmetrical, the central five bays projecting slightly and flanked by only one bay each
side; the first-floor windows (half the size of those
on the ground floor), which are conventionally
related to the bedroom floor levels, help impart
the air of a Palladian villa. This contrasts with the
entrance side, where the tall upper windows are
placed most inconveniently at floor level in the
bedrooms over the Hall, though it is an arrangement much enjoyed by the family dogs.

THE COACH-HOUSE AND STABLE BLOCK

The coach-house with its shallow-pitched roof and wide eaves was designed by Henry Hakewill for the fourth William Holbech in 1815–16. Hakewill also remodelled the older stable block nearby, giving it a similar roof and cupola (which contains an earlier clock).

THE OLD KITCHEN

There was once a service courtyard to the east, containing kitchens, laundry, dairy, brewery and other rooms, which was pulled down in 1930. This major work, together with the enlargement of the attic storey of the house and some ingenious internal alterations, is also attributed to Hakewill.

Henry Hakewill's design of 1816 for the forecourt gates

The forecourt gates

THE TERRACE WALK

WILLIAM HOLBECH'S TERRACE WALK AND ROMAN-STYLE COUNTRYSIDE

One of the most memorable features of Farnborough is the great terrace laid out by the second William Holbech along the ridge to the south-west, probably slightly before his remodelling of the house in the 1740s. John Loveday the antiquary notes in his journals that he 'rode on Mr W. Holbech's Terrace' in July 1742, the earliest record of it. A broad turfed ramp leads from the south front to an Ionic temple and a little oval pavilion, giving superb views, and thence to the obelisk three-quarters of a mile from the house, with an even wider panorama across the Warwickshire plain towards Stratford and the Malvern Hills. The Farnborough terrace marks a half-way stage between the formality of Bridgeman's raised walks at Stowe in Buckinghamshire, set out in lines, and the fully developed Picturesque style of the Rievaulx Terrace in Yorkshire. In many ways it can be regarded as a fulfilment of William Kent's approach to the Picturesque landscape garden, as seen, for instance, at Rousham in Oxfordshire.

The left side is closely planted with a protecting screen of beech and other hardwoods, sweet chestnuts and oaks with numerous shrubs, hollies, Portugal laurel and laurestinus in front. Old sketches and early photographs of the terrace fully mature show that in the nineteenth century the right-hand side closely resembled the left, making a sheltered walk. Here, William Holbech walked each day, so the story goes, to greet his brother who lived in the next village of Mollington.

On reaching the temples, he could pause and enjoy the views across the *ferme ornée* he had created, to the further landscape beyond. Because when he had returned from his Grand Tour inspired by the wonders of Italian art and landscape, William Holbech had set about re-creating a small piece of the Roman *campagna* here on the edge of Warwickshire, to try to emulate classical *arcadia*.

The term *ferme orné*, literally meaning ornamented farm, had been coined by an early exponent of landscape design called Stephen Switzer. He wrote that it was a way in which *both profit and pleasure may be agreeably mixed together* – so an agriculturally productive, though aesthetically improved, landscape that one might wander within for pleasure.

There are, consequently, views across pasture and arable fields and ponds to temples and the obelisk on the terrace. While many designed views are still discernible, and the characteristically classical Ionic Temple, Oval Pavilion and obelisk survive in good condition, some features have been lost.

Fascinatingly, however, recent archaeology has revealed the location and outline of some of these, including a summer house above the cascade, and an unusual terraced, circular feature known as an amphitheatre. This would have been specially planted so that it could have been walked within, but also viewed as a feature from the Hall.

Many of the original trees have inevitably succumbed to old age, disease or gales. But in 2014, Farnborough's park and agricultural areas qualified for funding from DEFRA's Higher Level Stewardship scheme. This is providing a major contribution towards replanting trees in accordance with both the 1772 estate plan and the Ordnance Survey's 1st series plan of 1886, which depicts many of the original trees when mature.

This scheme is also part funding repairs to park walls, restoration of the cascade and rebuilding of the weir on Sourlands Pool – the banks of which were cleared of dozens of overhanging alder trees over 2014/15. The fishing on that lake is let to an angling club.

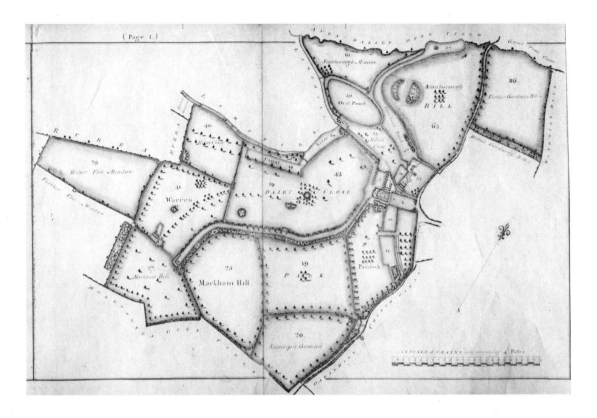

A map of about 1772, showing Farnborough Hall (1) and the second William Holbech's Terrace Walk of the 1740s, which stretches for three-quarters of a mile to the south-west of the house

Until the screen of trees that was planted to obscure the M40 extension was sufficiently grown, both the quiet of the Terrace and vista from it were sadly spoilt. But now, thankfully, the motorway's effect is far less injurious. However, the National Trust remains actively protective of Farnborough's setting within the wider landscape.

The immense labour involved in creating the Farnborough terrace was spelt out by the poet and parson Richard Jago in his topographical poem *Edge-Hill*, which was published in 1767:

Where the tall pillar lifts its taper head
Her spacious terrace, and surrounding lawns
Deck'd with no sparing cost of planted tufts,
Or ornamental building, Farnborough boasts.
Hear they her master's call? In sturdy troops,

The jocund labourers hie, and, at his nod
A thousand hands or [either] smooth the
   slanting hill
Or scoop new channels for the gath'ring flood,
And, in his pleasures, find substantial bliss.

Sanderson Miller of Radway probably gave his neighbour William Holbech decisive advice about the laying-out of the landscape at Farnborough, as he did for Lord Lyttelton at Hagley shortly afterwards. A mutual friend of all three was the poet William Shenstone, whose own landscape garden at Leasowes near Halesowen was an important pioneer of the Picturesque style – and Shenstone may well have been involved here too. A letter from him to Jago dated 14 December 1756 reads: 'Pray remember me to Mr Talbot [Sanderson Miller's client at Lacock], Mr Miller and Mr Holbech; should they call upon me next year, they will find my place better worthy of their notice.' Miller's own diary records frequent trips to Farnborough: in January 1750, for instance

(Right) A view across the parkland to the Ionic Temple

(evidently a mild month), he went 'to dine with Mr Holbech at Farnborough … drank tea at the summer house … and came home by moonlight'; while in July of the same year he brought over Lord Cobham, the owner of Stowe.

The buildings along the terrace were probably designed by Sanderson Miller and built by the Warwick mason William Hiorns, although it is intriguing to speculate whether William Jones, designer of the Ranelagh rotunda, may have had a hand in these pleasure buildings.

The Oval Pavilion

THE IONIC TEMPLE

The first to be encountered, about half-way along the terrace, is the Ionic Temple with a pediment supported by four Ionic columns, and loggia behind, flanked by two more half-columns. The building acts both as a sheltered viewpoint and (seen from below) as an eye-catcher against the dark trees behind. From the Ionic Temple the patchwork of fields and hedgerows stretching for miles across the country provides a quintessentially English scene, despite the M40. Nearer to, glimpses may be seen of the River Pool which William Holbech formed by remodelling two rectangular pools.

THE OVAL PAVILION

Further along the terrace and not far from the obelisk is a pavilion of a more unusual form: oval, with an open loggia at the bottom formed by four Tuscan pillars, and a carved stone staircase at the back leading to a delightful small 'prospect room' on the first floor.

The exuberant Rococo ornament applied to its domed ceiling and walls is in much the same vocabulary as that of the Drawing Room. Baskets of flowers, cornucopias and asymmetrical shell-work, or *rocaille* – which gave the Rococo style its name – are all here in abundance, picked out in white on a blue ground. The beautifully carved window frames with their original thick glazing bars should also be noticed.

(Right) The Ionic Temple

The Obelisk

THE OBELISK

The obelisk at the far end of the terrace was described by a visitor to Farnborough as early as 1746, so the date 1751 inscribed on its base may refer to the completion of the whole terrace by the 'thousand hands' of Jago's 'jocund labourers'. Both this visitor and Lady Newdigate, in her travel journal of about 1748, noticed yet another temple, which has since disappeared, on a hill between the obelisk and the main Banbury-Coventry road: the former described it as 'a summer house in the form of a pentagon, two stories high, with a balcony at the top ... the ornaments within being of carved wood', while according to the latter it stood 'upon five arches, in a little garden of flowering shrubs'. The summer-house is clearly marked on an estate map of 1772, which also shows that the terrace bordered with hedges forming semicircular bastions, as they do today, and again on Yates's map of Warwickshire, surveyed in 1786.

The obelisk unfortunately collapsed in 1823, but was rebuilt (as the inscription on it records), with the same high base, and particularly slender proportions. Future generations may be puzzled by the names of Italian prisoners carved into it during the last war, when Farnborough was used as an auxiliary military hospital – as it had been in the First World War.

THE GAME LARDER

Returning along the terrace, just before the final descent to the house, visitors reach a small path leading off to the hexagonal temple and game larder, probably designed by Miller and further adapted by Hakewill in the Regency period. Its four sturdy Tuscan columns provide a loggia overlooking a series of walled paddocks and some of the original seventeenth-century stewponds.

GRANNY'S WALK

Beyond the cedar tree, to the south-west of the house, a path (Granny's Walk) leads to the Rose Garden and alcove seat, on the site of a late Georgian orangery later used as a camellia house. A Georgian ice-house is tucked into the slope behind it. The path continues down to a cascade and grotto at the head of the lake, probably constructed in the 1740s. It formerly focussed on a summer-house on the mound above the cascade: its foundations have been discovered and await archaeological interpretation.

Parallel to Granny's Walk a delightful return walk to the Rose Garden has been created along a shrub lined path.

The Game Larder

This outstanding place, which survives as a complete concept from a fascinating moment in the development of English landscaping, is one of very few Grade 1 parks and gardens on the English Heritage Parks and Gardens Register. It is also one of the first parks to have received grant-aid from English Heritage, the Countryside Stewardship Scheme and, most recently, DEFRA's Higher Level Stewardship Scheme.

The view from Granny's Walk towards the Rose Garden

THE HOLBECH FAMILY

The name Holbech may originally have come from Holbek in Zeeland (part of Denmark), though the earliest recorded member of this branch of the family is thought to be Oliver Holbech, living at Holbeach in Lincolnshire in 1223. The family can certainly be traced back without a break to 1483, when Thomas Holbech was living at the White House, Fillongley, in north Warwickshire.

An entry of 1596 in the Fillongley parish register records the baptism there of Ambrose Holbech the elder, who became a well-known lawyer, and who had settled in the village of Mollington two miles south of Farnborough certainly by 1629. He eventually acquired most of the village and surrounding land, including the manor house.

Ambrose Holbech died in 1662, and was succeeded by another Ambrose, his eldest surviving son, of Mollington and Radstone Manor, Northampton, who bought Farnborough in 1683. His eldest son, William, married the daughter and co-heiress of William Alington and came to live at Farnborough after his marriage in 1692. He eventually succeeded to the three properties in 1701 and died in 1717.

He was followed by his son, also William Holbech, the connoisseur, who in the 1740s largely rebuilt the house and made extensive landscape improvements. After his death in 1771, a character sketch of him appeared in one of the county papers: 'His hospitality was according to the Apostle, without grudging, his integrity was unshaken, his benevolence was universal and his piety towards God was sincere.' His nephew, William, who succeeded in 1771, became MP for Banbury in 1792 and, in 1796, Deputy Lieutenant of the county. He married the daughter of Dr William Woodhouse of Lichfield, and their son, yet another William, married Lucy, the daughter of Oldfield Bowles of North Aston. They had many sons and daughters, but Charles, his third surviving son, succeeded in 1856. He married Laura Harriette, sister of Sir George Armytage of Kirklees Park in Yorkshire. Charles took Holy Orders and held the living of Farnborough, becoming Archdeacon of Coventry.

Archdeacon Holbech sold the Radstone estate and spent a great deal of money restoring the church at Farnborough, building a new aisle and spire to designs by Gilbert Scott. He also made a new road to the village of Avon Dassett one and a half miles away.

The Archdeacon had five sons and four daughters. The eldest, Walter, became a Colonel in the King's Royal Rifles and later one of the HM Royal Bodyguard. He married Mary Caroline, the daughter of Sir John Walrond of Bradfield, Devonshire. Another son became Bishop of St Helena and Tristan da Cunha, and the youngest,

A plaque in the Hall

Hugh, also took Holy Orders and later became vicar of Farnborough and a canon in the diocese of Coventry.

Walter Holbech predeceased his father, the Archdeacon, and in 1901 Farnborough was therefore inherited by his elder son, William. During the latter's minority, the estate was managed by Canon Hugh Holbech, who, like many of his forebears, was a great sportsman and a good judge of horse and hound, who also had a deep knowledge of country folklore.

William Holbech served in the Scots Guards in World War 1, and died of his wounds in October 1914. His brother, Ronald, then inherited and in 1915 married Catherine, the youngest daughter of Sir Leigh Hoskyns, 11th Bt. He was the last 'Squire' of Farnborough and in many ways a remarkable member of the family. Stricken with polio at the age of eight, he nevertheless succeeded to a great extent in overcoming this disability. He was an Alderman of the counties of Warwickshire and Oxfordshire, and Chairman of the Warwickshire Hunt for 31 years.

The eldest of Ronald Holbech's sons, Edward Ambrose, served with distinction as a Flight Lieutenant with the RAF during the Second World War, being awarded the DFC, but he was killed in an accident in 1945 on VJ Day. He had, however, already made a settlement on his only child, Anne, and his brother, Geoffrey. The house with 344 acres of surrounding land was acquired by the Treasury in lieu of death-duties in 1960, and transferred to the National Trust. At the same time Geoffrey Holbech gave an endowment. He and his late wife Elizabeth were then granted a lease, and thus continued to live at Farnborough.

Their daughter Caroline and her husband Alastair Beddall have now taken on the mantle of opening the Hall, which they do as well as pursuing their own independent careers.

The previously old fashioned kitchen has been updated by them for modern family use; and more

The Oval Pavilion in the nineteenth century

Farnborough from the south-west around 1860; watercolour by Mary Holbech

recently, they have installed a biomass boiler, too.

They have two sons – Max (b. 1993) and Angus (b. 1995) – one of whom, it is hoped, will continue to live in and run this important house. At the time of writing, however, Farnborough continues to be lived in by three generations of the family.

The principal furnishings including the sculpture and library had been left to Mr Holbech's niece, who kindly allowed them to remain in the house. These were bought in the late 1980s with the aid of the National Heritage Memorial Fund and the ever greater generosity of a private benefactor, who again stepped into the breach when the negro bust appeared at auction.

Rarely does a smaller-scale country house survive so completely with its original contents. Because of the high costs and limited scope for large numbers to view, government grants are increasingly unlikely to help save places such as Farnborough for the nation. The support of private individuals remains vital.

The plasterwork ceiling of the Oval Pavilion

(Left) The Terrace Walk in the nineteenth century

THE NATIONAL TRUST

- is a registered charity

- is independent of government

- was founded in 1895 to preserve places of historic interest or natural beauty permanently for the benefit of the nation

- relies on the generosity of its supporters, through membership subscriptions, gifts, legacies and the contribution of many thousands of volunteers

- protects and opens to the public over 350 historic houses and gardens, and 49 industrial monuments and mills

- owns more than 257,000 hectares (635,000 acres) of the most beautiful countryside and 775 miles of outstanding coastline for people to enjoy

If you would like to become a member or make a donation, please telephone 0344 800 1895 (minicom 0344 800 4410); write to National Trust, PO Box 574, Manvers, Rotherham S63 3FH; alternatively, see our website at www.nationaltrust.org.uk